BeHind ScHedule

MaLinda BaRbee

WESTBOW
PRESS®
A DIVISION OF THOMAS NELSON
& ZONDERVAN

This book is a work of non-fiction. Unless otherwise noted, the author
and the publisher make no explicit guarantees as to the accuracy of
the information contained in this book and in some cases, names of
people and places have been altered to protect their privacy.

Scripture quotations marked NIV are taken from the Holy Bible, New
International Version. NIV. Copyright 1973, 1978, 1984 by International
Bible Society. Used by permission of Zondervan. All rights reserved.

WestBow Press books may be ordered through booksellers or by contacting:

WestBow Press
A Division of Thomas Nelson & Zondervan
1663 Liberty Drive
Bloomington, IN 47403
www.westbowpress.com
1 (866) 928-1240

Because of the dynamic nature of the Internet, any web addresses or
links contained in this book may have changed since publication and
may no longer be valid. The views expressed in this work are solely those
of the author and do not necessarily reflect the views of the publisher,
and the publisher hereby disclaims any responsibility for them.

Any people depicted in stock imagery provided by Thinkstock are models,
and such images are being used for illustrative purposes only.
Certain stock imagery © Thinkstock.

ISBN: 978-1-9736-0564-5 (sc)
ISBN: 978-1-9736-0563-8 (e)

Library of Congress Control Number: 2017915362

Print information available on the last page.

WestBow Press rev. date: 06/14/2018

Table of Contents

Introduction

Have you ever been betrayed? While reading this book ponder the question and it will help you to realize just how deep betrayal can exist and the consequences both good and bad stemming from betrayal. This book will also help you to ponder how life, people including yourself may have betrayed your life in many ways but also this book will give you hope. There is hope in truth mainly because it is the truth which sets us free. There is hope beyond betrayal because there is purpose behind betrayal. Jesus was betrayed but yet His purpose had arrived.

The time had come. Judas one of Jesus disciples was about to betray Him with a kiss but for very little. Judas walked and supped with the King of Kings and the Lord of Lords over a span of time but ended up betraying the Most High for very little money offered by Jesus enemies for His capture. This was the small picture. The big picture is that Jesus had a purpose to fulfill and a destiny to continue to walk in to become Savior of those who accepted Him as the son of God. God is not dead and He is real and so is His son Jesus. Jesus is not an animated character many have heard about, He is a Savior. He came where we may be saved and delivered of what the enemy had planned for our lives. Satan the enemy had a plan for Jesus lives as He used Judas to carry out but the enemy didn't know it was to fulfill Gods perfect plan. So, Judas kiss of betrayal was perfect-timing because if Judas and Jesus enemies had not arrived when they did Jesus would have been BeHind ScHedule fulfilling His purpose. Judas betrayal led Jesus to carry His cross and drank of His cup which was given Him by His Father. Jesus was crucified on His cross where He died but only for a purpose, He went to hell and back to save us and gave us a future and hope and then He rose again in the third day. Mission Accomplished.

Who has betrayed you in your lifetime? Was it parent, relative, bully, stranger, co-worker, religious organization or self? Was it life's challenges, disappointments, failures which betrayed you? Whether it was sins of another such as a gang rape, an abusive spouse or sins of your own which life used to betray you there is still purpose in the betrayal but the enemy wants us to think otherwise. There are twist and turns in life which can seem to take us three steps backwards when we have taken six steps forward which can cause our journey to be longer than it has to be.

The Israelites went in circles in the wilderness for forty years because they were serving other gods (sin), perishing for the lack of knowledge, walking in generational curses and complaining about everything! "My people are destroyed for lack of knowledge: because thou hast rejected knowledge, I will also reject thee, that thou shalt be no priest to me: seeing thou hast forgotten the law of thy God, I will also forget thy children" (Hosea 4:6, NIV) The Israelites journey to their promise land should have only taken a few weeks but it took forty years. The enemy uses many tactics to detour us from our purpose and reaching our promise land but God can use those same tactics and many more to lead and guide us towards our purpose. Whether betrayed by person, sin, generational curses, trials and tribulations, disappointments or failure those betrayals lead us to fulfilling our purpose in life. Those betrayals lead us to carrying our cross, leads to the death of sins and generational curses being overcome in our lives and being resurrected with the mind of Christ Jesus working on the inside of us to fulfil our God given purpose. God still parted the Red Sea for the Israelites and the three steps backwards the enemy used for a setback God used for a setup! If you feel like you have been on a tedious journey in life and you are BeHind ScHedule get ready for your setback to propel you into your divine setup!

Prayer for Readers

Our Father which are in heaven and hallowed be thy name thy kingdom come thy will be done here on earth as it is in heaven. Father, I pray for every reader whom reads this book your will be done in their lives here on earth as it is in heaven. Father, whether the reader has endured molestation, alcoholism, drug addiction, unforgiveness, bitterness, depression or mental illness in any form or any other bondage or generational curses known or unknown within their family I pray you reveal yourself to this reader. I pray that your love becomes so evident in their lives your light will consume every dark area in their lives bringing them to wholeness in you. I pray you deliver every reader from hurt, pain, failure, disappointment, bitterness, unforgiveness or any issues of the heart where the wellsprings of life come from. Let their wellsprings overflow again and into the lives of their loved ones and everyone they meet! Father I pray each reader is delivered from the sins and sicknesses (generational curses) of their forefathers and delivered of every sin which easily besets them because they overcome by the blood of Jesus. He bore our sins and sickness on the cross. I pray that you will help them carry their cross which life has given them and they will carry their cross for their children, their children's children and generations to come will walk in freedom. You have given each person purpose in life which sometimes can only be brought forth through pain and suffering but let them know their life is not in vain. Father, reveal yourself to this reader and let them know if they have received your son Jesus Christ as Lord and Savior over their lives and believe they are free. Father, it is written whom the son sets free is free indeed. Father, I pray you allow this book to bless this reader to begin to walk in the freedom Jesus provided as He walked this earth, drank of His cup and fulfilled His purpose on the cross where we could live and not die and have eternal life. In Jesus name. Amen

Blink of an Eye

The older I became I realized that a part of me had been stolen, killed and destroyed by past chapters of my life and I soon realized that most of my life had changed within the blink of an eye. Many lives had been changed as I had started my own family and I could not pretend anymore because the cat had been let out of the bag and secrets came crashing out the closet door. Secrets which could not afford to go on any longer without other lives risk being jeopardized in the near future. Many of life's secret sins, generational curses and much more can only stand the test of time and they will be exposed! Although my life had been changed others were being spared of the wile tactics the enemy had prepared for my children and future generations. Satan only comes to steal, kill and destroy people's lives because he knows God created everyone with purpose "The thief comes only to steal and kill and destroy; I have come that they may have life, and have it to the full" (John10:10, NIV). Satan loves to operate in his purpose to abort the purpose of God's children any way he can accomplish his mission.

I had been defined by my past. Many people I had trusted had been put to blame in my eyes but in my heart I knew it was the enemy. I blamed satan and his wile tactics for abusing me, shaming me, finding me guilty for what had been done to me up to the current moment. It is then I realized I hadn't forgiven many people when my life began to unfold in misery. Misery of letting my past defeat me took me into battle mode against myself. The quest of being loved by men (although long-term relationships) was a test I failed along my journey until the battle always got the best of me and I would realize my past was beating up on me. My past had made me believe that no one could truly love me, I wasn't good enough for anyone, and I was spoiled and tainted. I accepted their love to be true but realized through relationship with God that false love never last. Did truth stop my quest? The answer is no. My past had rejected me and the battles I faced each day became lighter with co-dependent relationships tugging at me, controlled substances speaking to me, spinning around life wondering, why me? I could keep spinning around from day to day but it came a point I said, "I can take steps forward to get a few steps ahead" of my past which kept taunting me, defining me and defeating me over and over again in my mind.

Defeat was manifesting in my life because of what was stuck and brainwashed in my mind that my past controlled me and there was no way of escape. My past was lying to me which I had been believing the lies and my past made me believe my past owned me and there was no way to escape. "You owe me" my past would say, as I laid up from day to day in a co-dependent relationship and controlled substance (mostly marijuana for years until years later I graduated to crack cocaine) which took my pain away, temporary gratification which assisted in my past being abusive to me. My past was abusive to me, manipulating me, defining me and defeating me. The only question I had for my past was, why me? It wasn't until my future spoke to me when the blood of Jesus finally took hold of me, captured me from the destiny my past had planned for me and said, "Your past is a part of you because God had purpose for you and satan was trying to steal your purpose from you." I begin to understand

I was destined with purpose and that is why my past had been beating up on me trying to take control and ownership of me. My life changed with the blink of an eye with a simple revelation which came from up high. Still battling trying to escape my past and gain freedom, I would run into Jesus as I opened each door while battling or ran into closed doors but Jesus was there waging war in my mind bringing me to conclusion that satan had been lying to me. I didn't have to escape because Jesus served my time on the cross and I was free by the blood of Jesus. In my personal relationship with Jesus, He reminded me that I had a future in Him "For I know the plans I have for you, declares the Lord, "plans to prosper you and not to harm you, plans to give you hope and a future"(Jeremiah 29:11, NIV). My question all those years had finally been answered, why me?

At this time, I begin to ask God to repair me and I begin to seek Him with my whole heart "But seek first his kingdom and his righteousness, and all these things will be given to you as well" (Matthew 6:33, NIV). I wanted Him to restore me and make me whole where I could see the great things He had pre-destined for me and I became excited as He started sharing those details with me but not yet realizing the process is a tedious journey. It appeared freedom came and freedom left at times on my journey but in the midst Jesus had captured me and whom the son sets free is free indeed. His love was not replaceable, not comparable, and not quenchable with any other love I had ever known. I wanted more of His love but my past kept trying to take ownership of me. Freedom would not hang around when I would separate myself (freewill) from God by dipping and dabbing in the world of sin which beset me but Jesus was still carrying me (free indeed). I would ask Jesus to repair me, restore me and make me whole the way He had created me originally even when I felt far from Him I knew His hands were still on me. I know He had a plan for me and I desperately wanted to fulfill my destiny and He kept completing the good work He began in me along my journey and I trust in Him to continue to complete me until the day of Christ Jesus as promised me. "Being confident of this, that he who began a good work in you will carry it on to completion until the day of Christ Jesus" (Philippians 1:6, NIV). The high call is what I am running to obtain is achievable by His grace and mercy which He gives me over and over along my journey. "I press on toward the goal to win the prize for which God has called me heavenward in Christ Jesus" (Philippians 3:14, NIV).

Now, I see why my past continued to try and take ownership of me but without the Lord in my life there was no help for me. I had now learned how the enemy comes to steal, kill and destroy and did his best to suck all hope out of me. Somehow, someway the enemy would just keep attacking me with guilt, shame, fear and whatever else he could to sock it to me! Jesus was my only way of escape into my true reality by reminding me of the life He had planned for me. He died for me and the purpose which had been given to me was greater than me and I had to give Him my heart where He could lead me from day to day into complete freedom because without Him, I can do nothing. I would delight myself in Him and understood I could do nothing without Him including escaping the destiny my past which the enemy had planned for me.

Waging War

As time passed and I began to recognize the wile tactics of the enemy and his plan to hold me captive to my past, I began to pray. I prayed for every situation that trapped me in my past's closet. This led me to praying for many people including relationships the enemy had stolen or tainted. Prayer did not come easy to me at first because praying wasn't a habit I had developed. Prayer became a habit which I embraced once I discovered this was a habit which didn't consume me but liberated me of my past slowly but surely. Prayer opened doors and closed doors concerning my life's issues which I hadn't even noticed before. Prayer helped me to see change was on the way that things wouldn't stay the same way forever. Justification and vindication resulted from prayer and I was well on my way to recovery despite the process. Prayer was a light which brought me out of darkness as my Savior strengthened me in my areas of weaknesses which were actions and reactions of life from my past taunting me, defining me and defeating me. Prayer was the key and contributed to saving me from being defined, confined and defeated by my past forever. I begin to see victory like never before slowly but surely and I found out quickly Rome was not build in a day!

I am still in the mighty potter's hand because He is the potter and I am the clay and He can do whatever He pleases (Jeremiah

18:1-7, NIV). There is a thin line between victory and defeat because the more I prayed the more satan tried to knock me off my feet and the more he stood around corners trying to ambush me. Satan waited silently scheming up a plot to tempt me and see if he could take back victory of owning me and holding me bound to my past. He was successful many times but as the word says a just man falls seven times but we have sense to get back up again (Proverbs 24:16, NIV). I realized his wile tactics and he had actually tried to adopt me into the darkness with the lies of my past and he wasn't going to give up easy because he just knew his good thing would always last and he would abort Gods plan in my life. Suddenly my eyes begin to open more by developing a deeper relationship with God. I hadn't clearly understood before but was reassured troubles wouldn't last always as long as I let God's truth, His promises in the word and His love draw me nearer to Him because Jesus had saved me from my past which satan had pre-destined for me. I would see the salvation of the Lord in the land of the living (Psalm 27:13, NIV) because He promised to deliver me. It was finished.

It did not take long afterwards I had come into true knowledge that God was a real father and was alive that He was more than just a figment of my imagination or an icon what had been molded into my mind through only attending religious events during my childhood. God became real to me as the breath I breathed in everyday and God was actually on my side and had already won the victory needed for me to be saved from the hands of the enemy. This knowledge finally opened my blind eyes to see the real picture and it is when I took heed that the battle was never mine but the Lord's because satan had waged war with God long ago before I was even born. It now increased my awareness that if Jesus had a purpose and I had been born with a purpose that satan's purpose was just as real and was becoming clearer each and every day! Satan's purpose was to defeat me and keep me from walking in victory and freedom but thank God where the spirit of the Lord is there is liberty (2 Corinthians 3:17, NIV). It does not matter how it feels or appears we have freedom in God. Liberty is not actually free and I became aware of this knowledge more over time and it was only the blood of Jesus which kept me! I had a choice to hold onto liberty tightly or let it slip from my hands and enter back into the slavery the enemy had intended on keeping me. Every day I was fighting for liberty and there is a price to pay for liberty and that price is walking in our righteousness Jesus Christ had suffered to give me.

Walking out my righteousness had not come natural to me the enemy had set up boundaries for me but God had set a path for me and He was the light that kept attracting me. If I stayed on course of this path freedom captured me and when I detoured from the path and went a different course running back to my past, freedom soon slipped from me. Going in circles wasn't destined for me but it had become a habit that head easily beset me chasing after idols, sins and more which were trying to destroy me from co-dependent relationships to substance abuse. Every day was a battle but a new door God opened for me, His grace and mercy kept me and was constantly bringing me into new victories which Jesus had won for me. Satan's plan was to overtake me and it was clearer to me that he was stealing, killing and destroying me with a past which had overwhelmed me and tried to take me hostage on a day to day basis with fears and bondages which had captured and entangled me in a web too strong for me! Although satan used many attempts and he never gave up because he was always on his job Jesus was always standing in the gap for me reminding me over and over again that I had the victory. Victory is mine stood till in my heart even though troubles from the north, east, south and the west came and tried to rip me apart.

Satan's purpose is to wage war with the mind and if he can succeed he has accomplished a major part of his mission and that is to abort the mission God has put inside each of His creation.

As satan enclosed in on me by my hurtful past he drew me nearer to his arms, bounding me and gagging me with insecurities which led me back to my comfort zones. My comfort zones would be committing sins which were used to steal my identity, kill my warrior instinct (created in God's image Genesis 1:27, NIV), destroy my future God had planned for me and so much more. Satan was waging war and continually putting pressure on my by tempting me to escape my reality and just settle for those things which wouldn't benefit me, only for temporal gratification trying to cover up the pain within me. This life seemed easier. I had been shown my reality which was knowledge from God but freedom just kept slipping from my hands tearing me apart. There is a thin line between victory and defeat but every day that I took the right path Jesus was putting satan under my feet. Prayer was the weapon which kept lifting me, literally over the nights I was being lifted into new dimensions which kept good forces (angels watching over me Psalms 91:11, NIV) around me. Prayer was making my life clearer to me satan's purpose was sure but couldn't contain me because God had given me victory.

Hypnotic

B eing born into a world of sin (Psalm 51:5, NIV) didn't seem like victory was designed for me but as I begin to see in the spirit realm, the bigger picture I acknowledged there were two paths that had hypnotic power to lure me. It was my choice whether, I, the magnet would be pulled to or from the victorious life God had destined for me. The victorious life God had destined for me was a Kodak moment in my visions compared to the nightmare of my past that had been defining me and defeating me. My background of hurt, pain, rejection and other contributing factors were present but when I chose to be lured towards the light of my salvation, my background, and my past didn't not stand a chance to continue to stand against me. If my God was for me who in the world could be against me (Romans 8:31, NIV)? The answers is not anyone and not even my past that had been defining me and defeating me. I had to start making choices day by day to be lured towards the path that was not meant to destroy me but my background didn't make it easy for me.

Trying to escape the horror always caused sorrow that would cause me to be tossed to and fro and upside down until again, I would hit rock bottom in a pit of despair. My background, my past was back to haunt me. The enemy would once again come back to take ownership of me, manipulating, abusing, defining and defeating me by my past. Each time I stepped and was lured towards the destiny God had created for me and opened up to God as my best friend, let Him take my heart captive where it should be, the enemy would get desperate and try to take my liberty from me. Knowing all the right buttons to push and holding some of the keys to my mind and heart, the enemy still knew how to work against me, using my background, my past against me and constantly defeating me.

My arms wide open to relationships but really not knowing love and these relationships were introducing me to things which were not good for me without love being present in my company. I was being lured into the hand of the enemy, head on a platter, where satan had plans to devour me, devour me from lack of knowledge of what was taken place within me, my past, my background had a hold on me. My past knew I just wanted harmony, to be loved just for me, trust and rejection free in every relationship presented to me. I had complexes from my past which stagnated my intimacy most of my life. I could not relax and completely open up to anyone and it took years for me to trust that person and become very comfortable. This caused tension in most of my relationships although a superficial love was obvious there was not complete satisfaction which caused rejection to increase within me. My past was still manipulating, abusing, defining and defeating me but God had His grips on me.

He wouldn't let me get too far gone for He had charged my angels to keep me in all my ways. God had gone to war for me and although my past taunted me, God had made ways of escape for me every time bringing me back to reality. Reality, nothing compared to the promise God had for me and I refuse to not walk in my identity or my destiny. Created in God's image, I knew although the odds were against me, I had the victory! Back to Eden I was headed, back on top of the world, living victorious with God on my side. I was not worried about tomorrow because tomorrow had its worries of its own. I'd lie down in the green pastures where God had led me, I was a secure sheep because I was being led by the hand of the Almighty who had great plans for me. Jesus would bring the sunshine into my life on a daily basis despite the challenges. His mercies are new every morning and it would be like a sweet kiss every time His mercies would show up unannounced, He was courting me, loving me and drawing me nearer. What kind of love had found me? This love was strange but real and I wanted to keep it near. This love that lured me drew me nearer and nearer but would sometimes feel distant because of my past trying to come near, trying to claim ownership year after year. My past still manipulating, abusing, defining and defeating me and was causing me to walk in fear.

Fear would take hold of me during my journey and I didn't want to be alone but once again I would enter my comfort zone. I'd begin to drift into sins which were luring, exciting and boring, nothing new but old self-gratifying the flesh, numbing the pain which led down Dead End Boulevard. I am grateful God comprehends the reasons I would resort back to my comfort zones. He understands you too! If satan could destroy me then he could destroy my tree, my family. Satan's goal was to use my past and background constantly to steal, kill and destroy purpose and destiny which was designed to fulfill the great plan of God to put satan under His feet and for our good, a greater good. We each have a purpose just as Jesus to be carried out to take satan's kingdom down!

The mission is not impossible because with God all things are possible (Matthew 19:26, NIV). The enemy makes the mission seem impossible in the natural eyes but in the spirit God reminds us the joy of the Lord is our strength and Emmanuel is God with us carrying us into victory. Being born into a world of sin was the path set before me but with God all things are possible and despite all the odds against me I seen in sight, I knew I had the victory. My past and issues of the heart may have been weapons meant to destroy me but Jesus took the nails in His hands to redeem me, therefore His grace and mercy endures forever in life, freeing me of sin that so easily beset me (Hebrews 12:1, NIV). My past was a part of me manipulating, abusing, defining and defeating me from time to time but I, the magnet was constantly being lured to the light of my salvation, my Savior Jesus Christ who was carrying me.

Blazing Torch

Generations before me carried the same burdens, carried the same crosses and this helped liberate me from day to day from my daily experiences as I begin to understand generational curses. I discovered I did not have to continue to walk with a curse torch and neither should have the generations before me. I may have been born into generational curses which were meant to consume me but every day I was a step closer to my true identity even when my true identity tried to escape from me and become swallowed up in the test which was facing me. Day to day I thought I just couldn't go on raising four children with all the challenges but that was just a few of the lies satan was feeding me. The curse was haunting me as I lay sleeping in my bed, sleeping in my bed of tears wondering over and over again, why me? Why was gravity weighing down on me, sleeping in my bed with a lot going through my head wondering, why had life made these choices for me, before there was a me? Generational curses trying to overtake me, day to day I came to see it wasn't going to be easy for me.

The father I had known was long gone and unfortunately I never really knew my real father until it was too late to form a true bond. Now my children and I were left all alone with men who didn't know their identity in God at all to live this life without the privilege of having and maintaining a happy home

as portrayed in the Huxtable family! The generations before
carried burdens and had passed those burdens to me like a torch
I was holding and running through my life with generational
curses following me like a shadow meant to consume me. Later
to my amazement to realize I did not possess the full knowledge
of generational curses but God was constantly bringing me into
the light. God shines the light on darkness in our lives for His
glory and it is up to us to choose to not let the enemy be the
author and finisher of our story. Sleeping in my bed suffering
depression with many thoughts running through my head as I
was trusting Jesus to be my daily bread. It was the daily bread
that helped me to see that God had prepared a way for me to
come out the slimy pit that satan had staged for me sink in
without any grips to pull up, up and up. My daily bread helped
me to focus from day to day experiences sleeping in my bed with
many thoughts running through my head. I know this wasn't
the plan for me but generational curses were trying to go before
me to destroy my destiny. Working was my second nature and
through being a work-a-holic those curses wouldn't be exposed
as quick and by working hard I had hoped to change my destiny!
I discovered quickly working was just a cover up that would
swallow me up and contribute to generational curses consuming
my family and me and led me to sleeping in my bed with many
thoughts running through my head because I still wasn't getting
anywhere. Sleeping in my bed became a comfort zone, a place
my mind could roam freely and not be distracted. My thoughts
didn't come easy because my generational curse torch was being
carried by me, but not deliberately. If it wasn't for the Lord on
my side, pulling, tugging and saving me from a day to day war I
would have just slept in my bed and asked the Lord to spare me.
I would have asked the Lord to spare me from the pain of the
curses which had come through my door, a door which had been

opened generations before me. The door had been opened by generations before me but every day I had a decision to make to go left or let God take me to the right. I made some good, some bad decisions and some I didn't have to make because former generations had already claimed its territory in which route I would possible take. If it wasn't for the Lord leading me and guiding me from day to day my children and my life would stay the same way. Sleeping in my bed with many thoughts running through my head I had to get past my comfort zone and claim the victory in my life on a daily basis with God on my side. With God, I was making better choices daily because I wanted to please my love, Jesus. The Lord of my life was giving me strength to take the good with the bad and the ugly. The Lord's grace and mercy brought me through my daily battles even with all the thoughts which were running through my head.

Raising four children and entering co-dependent relationships created instant fear, fear led to failure and the enemy stayed battling in my mind, his battleground. This led me to constantly sleeping in my bed with many thoughts going through my head. Generational curses vary and there is usually more than one but I knew depression was the first to give me a clue because depression was trying to consume me but God was always there to deliver me.

My good days outweighed my bad days and I was glad God was not just another man there and I could always hear Him reminding me that trouble didn't last always. He hadn't brought me this far to leave me and He was always present with me. I begin to understand the choices that had been made in my life for me by generations before me but God took the burden from me and let me know that the generational curses would not consume me. Satan's plan was overturned when Jesus my Savior died for me, resurrected He saved my family and me and we had been given the victory through Him. Jesus was constantly leading me beside still waters ensuring me that I had the victory and He as working the good, the bad and the ugly out to make a better me. Thank God for saving me were the thoughts which began going through my head eventually as I lay in my bed.

Staying Anchored

Daily reminders came frequently of the decisions that I had made and the decisions that had been made for me by those generations before me which led to my life not being established on a solid foundation capable of instantly carrying me into victory. Past generations had been defeated by satan and he was still trying to maintain his championship victories. There was always a battle before victory but in time I had realized the battle was the Lord's and He had paid for every wrong decision, hurt, disappointment, mistake, failure and more in full. My past had defined me and was trying to defeat me which was constantly creating problems for me but my soul had become anchored in the Lord and I realized He was truly there for me. Every day there was a battle which tried to take me out, wipe out the faith I had and increase doubt. Every time God brought me out and it helped me to get to know His love more as I went about everyday trying to figure my life out. While I was trying to figure things out God was constantly showing me He had already worked things out. It was a constant battle then and sometimes a minor battle now to be patient on and in God.

I always had an unfaithful button during times of affliction, trials and tribulation. As soon as the going became tough I would get going and it has taken God's love and patience towards me to overcome unfaithfulness, one day at a time and afflictions.

He might not come when we want Him but He sure is on time, every time! I would have to let the praise out because He always showed Himself worthy! I begin to count the trials, tribulations and temptations all joy because I realized God was for me and not against me and victory was mine. Those battles have always helped challenge me and push me closer to my destiny and God strategically was completing His good work He had begun in me all along. It never failed, one season I would be white as snow and the next season I would have fallen back into muddy sin. Through it all, God had covered me by His son's blood my freedom still would remain. I just had to come back to reality and hit the refresh button and walk in my freedom once again because whom the son sets free is free indeed. Freedom was always a choice away even though at that time I really didn't understand that Jesus had paid the cost for my complete freedom once I accepted Him into my life as my Lord and Savior. I could walk in freedom or be bound in sin.

God was turning my battles into victory, delivering me surely but slowly from a past that had been defining me and defeating me by His unfailing love. God was courting me, chasing me and cleansing me one day at a time. I begin to fall in love with a love that was bigger than me and I begin to believe and accept He had a greater plan for me without a doubt. The more I begin to focus on my personal relationship with God the more chaos in my life begin to increase in various areas of life, from co-dependent relationships to family problems. I knew satan was trying to pin me down and drown me in a pool of trials and tribulations which would rise on a daily basis. Some decisions which I had made while spiritually blind or decisions which I suffered from because of generational curse decisions made before me. These decisions which stemmed from my past were trying to define and defeat me, constantly following my children and me. My children and I had troubles on every side and some seen and some unseen but with God on my families side we survived daily under God's wing.

Remaining under God's wing is what was keeping me because the enemy doesn't fight fair and his tactics are endless. Satan was constantly trying to cause despair, my children and I living from here to there because of the fear that had rested in my heart which was rooted from failure, hopelessness and despair. Situations I couldn't get a grip on and problems I couldn't face led me to wallowing in self-pity not recognizing my God was still there! Most days lying in my bed with many thoughts running through my head, paralyzed by fear that things just didn't look good and those things were not meant to get any better from there. Wondering, if things were going to get better, hoping things were going to get better but what else must I endure? When would things change for the better? I had seen a part of the picture but the whole picture was never clear and I couldn't recognize God's hand was half-closed for a reason, it was never meant for me to see everything in His hands concerning my life at one time. I just had to sit back and trust God and know that He would perfect those things which concerned me in His time.

Again, my soul had been anchored which led me to continue to trust in God and I began to count all my trials and tribulations all joy deep down in my heart each day even when there was nothing to smile about. Developing this habit trusting (Proverbs 3:5-6, NIV) in God with all my heart and leaning not to my own understanding and letting him direct my path no matter what helped me to experience on a daily basis that God was truly working all things good and bad out for my good and it made life better knowing my life was in His hands. " And we know that in all things God works for the good of those who love him, who have been called according to his purpose" (Romans 8:28,

NIV). Trusting in God is when He began to confirm to me more that He had a greater plan for me and He was taking my faith from glory, to glory, to glory for His glory. Life wasn't grand but my God was and I began to know that He was capable of the impossible! Although, my past kept on trying to take ownership of me, God's hands were on my life and I knew the plans He had were not to harm me but prosper me and He had been keeping me, leading me and guiding since birth. In the midst of it all, I could walk in the freedom of knowing that God was carrying me, carrying me right into my destiny which He had planned for me.

Knock Knock!

S atan tries to master the games and the wile tactics which he uses to throw God's children off course but God is a game changer. God uses some of the same games and wile tactics the enemy uses against us for us by the end of the game, being the game changer. Satan will always knock on the door of the heart to see if someone is home. "God didn't give us a spirit of fear but power, love and a sound mind" (2 Timothy 1:7, NIV) . Once fear came and entered my heart satan would make himself at home and stay for breakfast, lunch and dinner! While he was there he would always remind me of the should of, could of and would of's and all this issues of my past, all the mistakes that I had made and would just rub it in trying to take back ownership and define and defeat me with my past.

The struggle continued but my soul had been anchored in the Lord and I had become to know my identity just a little bit more than the day, week, month and year before. The game was changing and God was making me victorious winner though Christ Jesus because without Him, I am nothing and can do nothing. Satan, the "wanna be" game master has lost his master key once again and God begin to breathe life back into me, His son Jesus Christ is the way, the truth and the life (John 14:6, NIV). Jesus, my Savior stepped in the game and was saving me from satan being able to use my past to mold me into the way he saw fit for me, defining and defeating me by my past, satan no longer had permanent victory over me. Satan had a temporary license and it was soon to expire because Jesus had declared victory for me and over me on the cross, Jesus said, "It Is Finished" (John 19:30, NIV) and this goes for your life too! Whatever the enemy is using to keep you from walking in the purpose that God has placed inside of you "It is Finished" and you shall come forth as pure gold.

"It is Finished" was engraved in my heart like a tablet and whether it was a good day or a bad day I knew it was only the blood of Jesus which had already finished my day victoriously defeating satan every step of the way. Even on the cloudy days the "Son" would still be shining but it satan could get in my mind and stay and cause me to doubt Jesus then he would have been able to use his temporary key/license and play tricks on me. Jesus would remind me of His faithfulness and past victories and future victories which could excite me, quench my thirst and renew my hope. Just as Job, satan thought I would curse God but God quenched my thirst in the midst of each desert and gave me hope and yet did I trust in the Lord! Tossed to and fro is what satan wanted to see but God is a game changer and He caused delusions in the satan and let him see what he wanted to see concerning me. Satan seen me faint and weary because he always seem to frustrate the good plans for me or control my day from day but God seen me holding on, soul anchored in Him, trusting and growing in Him from day to day. From day to day I begin realizing my past could not hold me, couldn't keep me living there because Jesus had fulfilled His purpose on the cross and rising from the tomb and He held the master key to my destiny. Jesus held the key to me crucifying me flesh daily and walking in the freedom He had bought and paid in full with His blood for me. Satan desires for us to have the same future as him.

Satan constantly reminding me of my past but he had lost his ownership of defeating me and defining me with my past and now I can remind him of his future. Satan went from being God's chief musician, walking in his purpose for the Kingdom of God, to being God's enemy, walking in his purpose for the Kingdom of darkness! I came to the conclusion, that I was a friend of God's and an enemy of mine is an enemy of God's and satan had been made my footstool because he is under Jesus feet and I have been released from his hook. I can swim, float and be free in Jesus because satan's hook can't contain me because there is power in the blood of Jesus. Amazing grace how sweet the sound that saved a wretch like me, I once was lost but now I am found was blind but now I see, rescued from satan's net trapped and bound by defeat, I have the victory! I see day to day and more and more how satan used my past to defeat me and define me playing tug of war with Jesus concerning everything about me. Jesus winning each battle giving me victory, constantly. So all along, the only thing satan was doing was being used as a time machine because he was my slingshot towards walking in my purpose on the way to my destiny.

I was lost but now I am found and I was blind but now I see that greater is coming and I will see God's plans for me.

I will fulfill the purpose God has assigned me just as Jesus fulfilled His purpose. It was my past, my mistakes that satan used against me that became the bridge which begin to lead me to freedom and victory. I begin to appreciate when satan reminded me of my past because God would always show me a glimpse of my future. The big picture is all that begin to matter to me as I continued to seek God because His promise was becoming more real to me. "Seek ye the kingdom of Heaven first and its righteousness and all the other things shall be added" (Matthew 6:33, NIV).

Just Do It!

God is the Alpha and the Omega and everything including our life has a beginning and an end. The beginning of any family stems from the root of the tree and flourishes to the end and each branch forms generation after generation. In comparison, the beginning of my life which is stemmed to my past became the root of my tree which foundation was my past concerning my childhood in being molested compared with many other lives and their roots and past which altered and pre-determined our lives because of previous generational curses, afflictions and more. Generational curses derive from sinful decisions which had been made by our forefathers such as great grandparents, grandparents, parents which are all branches of the tree and even our decisions affect future branches which can pave the way for many future victims. Generational curses are mixed in the root (beginning of our lives) and will try and take over the entire tree (past, present and future of our lives and future generations) if not severed before we have reached our complete life span (our end) and the generational curse then goes to the next generation (other branches such as our children and great grandchildren) to take ownership, rule, reign, define and defeat future generations with the same curses. Instead of a beautiful forest (Like the Garden of Eden, Family growth) satan causes generational curses to cause forest fires within family trees because of generational curses to spread rapidly until a pioneer of the family say's enough is enough and it's time to put the fire of generational curses out. The torch stops here!

We were all born into a world of sin (world full of spirits) ready to take ownership or devour our lives at birth. My childhood like many others' and maybe even yours had been tainted. As I look back over my life when I was in my late twenties I realized that satan is also a strategic god and he knew just when to enter into a person's life (childhood) to begin the process of stealing, killing and destroying. At this point, I had already just about had enough! Enough was enough and I begin to have zeal to diligently seek God where He could begin to take the pain and misery away. In my mother's womb satan tried to kill me with tuberculosis and also sowed seeds of rejection while I was in the womb by being separated from biologically father before birth. The separation from biologically father before birth was just another plot of the enemy to not be capable of establishing a firm foundation in a two parent home just as many other children. Satan comes to steal, kill and destroy but our God is a refuge, strong tower, father, mother, friend and more and He came where we could all have life more abundantly (John 10:10, NIV). We may have been born into generational curses and a world of sin but Jesus died where we do not have to live or die in the generational curses pre-destined to consume us.

Jesus died where we could walk on water, we do not have to keep drowning as the enemy intended for us and our families to in various life trials and tribulations of the past, present or future. Change is easier said than done! The healing and deliverance process is continuous but worth every bit of it and there is a thin line between the past and present. How could satan take the past and defeat and define us in our present? Simple, satan had the upper hand he had been using our families past generational curses for decades and maybe even centuries against generation after generation. This is why family sins and strongholds are called generational curses. There is a huge gap between past and future but the enemy is always trying to build a bridge to cause future generations to walk on the bridge of curses instead of the bridge of blessings, faith, hope, love, freedom and more but God said, "Where the spirit of the Lord is there is liberty" (2 Corinthians 3:17, NIV).

Satan knows our future generations matter, we matter and we can walk in our liberty! "For I know the plans I have for you," declares the Lord, "plans to prosper you and not to harm you, plans to give you hope and a future" (Jeremiah 29:11, NIV). It doesn't matter what has taken place or hasn't taken place in our lives God uses those battles as slingshots from our past to our future and the enemy becomes our footstool as generational curses are broken by God using pioneer family members who are determined to keep satan where he belongs and that is under our families, our futures feet by defeating the sin in our own lives. Working out our own salvation with fear and trembling and resisting sin/satan will begin to cause families to reign victoriously by the blood of Christ Jesus.

Recognizing a generational curse in families is being capable of identifying the sins, strongholds and bondages within a family from A to Z such as alcoholism, voodoo (any form of witchcraft), sexual immorality, Fear (fear of all kinds), pride, rejection and more. Recognizing all forms of generational curses in one's family is the key to taking the victory back which was paid in full by Jesus Christ fulfilling His purpose. Walking in sin/disobedience gives satan a right to operate within a family limits (like city limits) to continue to achieve his wile tactics of stealing, killing and destroying from generation to generation. Recognizing and identifying with these factors is the first step which will lead families to freedom, freedom leads to victory and victory is ours! We have to tell satan to get thee behind our families once and for all. Satan is our slingshot into our destiny once we acknowledge and agree that Jesus has taken all his rights away but we must choose which God we shall serve. God is a jealous God and satan knows the only way he has a right to enter into our lives and continue generational curses in our lives is for us to remain in sin, serving him and other gods. Other gods can range from money, material items, people and more! Serving anything but God can give satan his key back and he can come home and enter our lives to steal, kill and destroy at any time hindering generations after generations.

Used Weapons

S atan knows he can steal our purpose, kill our dreams and destroy our destiny if he can continue to define and defeat us with our past, pain, hurts, disappointments, betrayal, heartbreaks and many more issues of the heart. The word tells us to not put our trust in mere princes (Psalm 146:3, NIV) (people) because they would fail us every time and in most cases it is people or ourselves which creates issues of the heart. Don't put trust in that person viewing your application whether for job or housing, the judge viewing the evidence against you or whatever the case may be. Satan knows the word of God but to continue to define and defeat us with our past he would have us to be ignorant and as mere humans we are meant to err and we should not put so much trust in people but we do. Satan knows as children we are ignorant of this knowledge and we trust adults until we are taught we can't trust strangers but we trust just about every adult which can cause us to perish and also perish spiritually in many ways which is what the enemy counts on. We have to trust God to trust others. Through most of our lives we can identify with experience and remaining focused on the hurts, pains, abuse, betrayal and more which derived from various relationships.

In those relationships satan comes to steal our confidence, worth, self-love, identity and more. Satan comes to kill our hope, joy, faith every day and he comes to destroy our goals, visions over and over again. Any wile tactic or weapon he can out of his bag and throw our way is usually something he has already used in the past. If it worked in the past he counts on the same weapon to work again and he is closer to his goal of stealing, killing and destroying our destinies. Satan always know how to provoke me by bringing up my past of being molested and abused by people very close to me, not being the best single parent (not being properly parented myself) or whatever part of my past he could sock to me. Although, my true identity had been stolen and the root of my problem stemmed from generational curses such as mental illness (depression) and being sexually and physically abused the enemy would try and plant seeds in my head that it was all my fault and nothing would ever change in my life. Satan had tried to convince me that my life would continue to be defeated and defined by my past! Satan is out to abort the entire plan of God in our lives and this did not begin with us! Satan tried to abort the plan of God in Jesus life and tempted Jesus but Jesus used the word against satan right back, game changer! God will give us the word to stand against satan too and we have to apply it to our lives. Once we start applying the word to our lives it becomes a habit, a good habit! The enemy will try and steal our mind renewing habits too but Jesus overcame the thief!

Remember, we are replacing "satans habits" with "God habits." Satan counted on me to not decide that enough was enough! I was not going to continue to let him manipulate my mind into thinking that I had to settle and be a prisoner to my past for the rest of my life and to let generational curses consume my life, my children and my grandchildren's lives. Enough was enough! Once, I begin to seek ye the kingdom of Heaven first and His righteousness as (Matthew 6:33, NIV) mentions and trust God for His plans for my life it was no turning back. Even when I slipped and fell (Proverbs 24:16, NIV) God picked me up and placed my feet back on solid ground once again, I would continue on my journey. I would continue the journey to take back everything that the enemy had stolen form me and everything he was trying to steal from me. Pursing, overtaking and recovering all the enemy had stolen but not only from me but from generations before me. It is not an easy task and not what I expected at all but through it all I learned to depend on Jesus and trust in His word. God was always taking my faith and still takes my faith from glory, to glory to glory for His glory. It's not about us but about Jesus and the Bible tells us we would go through just as much as Jesus suffered.

We may go through hurts, pains, betrayals, disappointments, failures and more in life but in remembrance and according to the word of God we must suffer just as Jesus suffered. Our suffering does not compare to one day reigning with Him gloriously in Heaven. Satans main objective was to abort Jesus purpose from Him and tempt Jesus to fail His mission which was to become our Savior. What is your purpose? We each was created with a purpose and satan tempts us throughout our lives with everything under the sun to get us to remain ignorant that we have a purpose or continue to run from our purpose. Through this satan can continue to defeat and define us by our past and steal our true identity and keep if for himself. Jesus Christ is our Savior, His true identity and if He had let satan tempt Him out of His purpose there would be no you and I today to have passed the torch too! Are you ready to take your torch of generational curses and replace with generational blessings and pass this torch to your future generations? You have purpose inside of you ready to spread a fire and it's time to pursue, overtake and recover all and walk into your destiny!

Faces

To be capable of pursuing, overtaking and recovering all the enemy has stolen or trying to steal there are chains which must be broken and vary in each individual's life but many experience alike issues. It is tedious process in most cases but worth it and God deserves all the glory and He helps us to recognize the many faces along our journeys. He gave His only begotten Son. These chains and faces can range from generational curses, childhood problems to lacking a relationship with God and making Him Lord over our lives. Whatever the links in the chain represent which caused the chain to keep adding links must go because the chain is what satan uses to take one hostage and control their life, making one appear like a puppet. Just a few examples below:

Generational Curses

Whether it's alcohol to sexual immorality generational curses can potentially travel from one generation to the next generation to hold each generation captive. God said, (Hosea 4:6, NIV) His people perish for the lack of knowledge and most people think of generational curses as freedom (freewill) or even fun but generational curses are meant to detour life into the wrong direction. The Israelites were detoured in the wrong direction and were in the wilderness for forty years because of serving other gods/sin. It was only God whom led them out of the wilderness and through the Red Sea to where they should be. Once we begin to give up our freedom and fun in life is when God can begin to lead us in the right direction and we begin to experience true freedom because who the son sets free is free indeed and we are no longer captives of the enemy. Our future generations are liberated as well through a courageous and unselfish act to pursue, overtake and recover all the enemy has stolen generation after generation.

Childhood Hurts, Betrayals and More

The word says, "Train up a child in the way they should go and when they are old they will not depart from it" (Proverbs 22:6, NIV). Even when we go our own separate directions apart from God in life once we have been introduced to Him, we always seem to be led back to Him. His staff is always guiding us (His sheep) back to Him (pasture). Satan loves to train up a child too and he counts on children to be trained up with a lack of relationship with God just as with a lack of relationship with natural parents for his own good. What better way to train up a child than to take the child's mind and heart into his own hands while they are yet too young to understand what is really going on in the spiritual realm? This allows satan to be capable of leading and guiding the young hearts in the direction he chooses for them. Satan has the upper hand being capable of achieving his goal of detouring a young child's life and maybe it was yours by stealing, killing and destroying bits and pieces of a soon to be an adult individual's life by corrupting their life in the beginning.

Fear

Fear and faith are opposite and each has their own unique benefits within each realm. Fear and faith are just like a positive and negative battery. Benefits can be obtained by possessing both but one will result to a negative (fear) outcome and one will result to a positive (faith) outcome which will either result to life or death concerning that situation. Yes, we can reap benefits from having fear but they are not a reward. There are no rewards for having fear because satan reaps the benefits when we harbor fear because God did not give us a spirit of fear but power love and sound mind. When we walk in faith God continues to take our faith from glory, to glory to glory and we reap the benefits (promises of God) which is all for His glory. During a race there is first place, second place and third place rewards for those who win the race. There are no benefits for those whom did not win but they can still pat themselves on the back if they at least finish the race. There are no benefits for those who start the race but give up halfway in between not unless it was a medical emergency then their lives may have been saved. Satan counts on us to not start the race or give up in the race because of fear and various types' fears but it is really not how you run the race but that you strive to reach the prize of the high call (Philippians 3:14, NIV). Fear leads to failure and this is what the enemy desires from our lives the most. Failure is another link added to the chain of life which leads many to be oppressed and unable to hope and see past the failure which results to hopelessness.

Failure is unlimited and Failure's eyes never sleep and Failure is always looking for a person to enter their homes (spirit) that maybe sleep or slumbering due to many factors in life such as being without adequate knowledge, walking in fear and more. Failure likes to enter through one's spirit during the weakest moments in life but is not limited to entering in strong moments of life. Failure comes to break a person and does not have a preference but only goal is to try and knock the life (goals, dreams, ect.) out of you. From single parents to many wealthy people on earth there have been moments of fear which have caused temporary or permanent failure within an individual's life. Fear is unlimited and ranges from the least to the greatest of circumstances and satan does not want us to be capable of detecting all fear. Single parents can fear something as minor as not getting a much needed check in the mail to being evicted from not getting the check in the mail. What is going to happen? They are not going to get the check and they are going to be evicted because instead of having faith they chose fear. Whatever the individual fear can possible happen. Same scenario with individual a renewed mind standing on the promises of God and relying on God to supply all their needs according to His riches and glories in heaven. God comes in right on time, every time and it is true He may not come when or how we want Him to come but He will come right on time, Fear or Faith? Fortunately, we have all experienced both which God works out for our good.

Celebrities and many others have committed suicide because of fear stemming from the least of things such as exposure, disappointments, tragedies and more. These factors caused these people to be uncomfortable with the outcome and felt as if they did not have a sense of control of the situation. The Bible says, "Blessed are those whose confidence is in the Lord" (Jeremiah 17:7, NIV) and many who commit suicide give up or do not begin to trust in the Lord but themselves. It seemed better to take their own life than put their life in God's hands and trust Him. Satan counts on one having a lack of knowledge, pride and more as long as he gets the glory out of this lost life. Fear clearly understands its purpose and sole intentions are to cause the person to fear knowing whatever the person fears will be accomplished. Faith also understands its purpose and that is why we have dominion over fear because Jesus overcame the world including fear. We begin to soar like the eagles God created us to be when we can master the art of choosing faith over fear.

For the person fearing loss, that is shall be and whatever the loss is. It can be a job, a car, a home, battle, etc. and fear has accomplished its goal. The "fear bullies" can become fatal bullets which end up causing one to commit suicide or a crime because of lack of faith or trusting in self, everything and everyone except God. A negative outcome is exactly what the enemy counts on because if he can break one, he will but if he can collect a soul in the situation he will collect the soul, pass go and go straight to hell. Fear has many faces and we have to ask God to show us where the fear is in our lives because fear comes in many faces fear will keep knocking trying to get in. Fear's root is strengthened each time it enters and is watered or applied to our lives instead of having faith. If God can take our faith from glory, to glory, to glory then satan can take fear down the same road! Fear would not only turn into a tree at this point but an entire forest and spread throughout the forest like a forest fire for a lifetime.

Identifying the fear is the beginning of the process to telling satan "fear get thee behind me" and begin standing on the promises of God's word. Speaking God's word where there would be fear and letting the situation or problem know what God's word says about it. It may look like the bills are not going to be paid but God said, "He would supply all of our needs according to His riches and glories in Heaven" (Philippians 4:19, NIV). The doctor may say, "you have six months to live" but the Bible says, "you shall live and not die and declare the works of the Lord" (Psalm 118:17, NIV) and with the word we are given an option to believe two reports. Whose report are you going to believe? The enemy counts on us not to use the word of God during a storm because most storms come in and destroy before there is time to prepare to evacuate. The word says, "When satan comes in like a flood God will rise up a standard against him" (Isaiah 59:19, NIV) but fear can and is meant to paralyze one in the midst of the storm and the storm has the victory! We must remember that if God be for us who in the world can be against us (Romans 8:31, NIV) and God had already worked it out for our good. As Job said, yet will I trust in the Lord (Job 13:15, NIV)!

Anger, Bitterness and Resentment

We all experience anger during our lifetime and plenty of times especially before we learn to overcome anger but if we let anger build up in us over the years it is not healthy for us. Anger is worse than high blood pressure, high cholesterol, clogged pipes and anything we can think of that builds up or can build up! Anger is so dangerous when we allow it to build up that the Bible states we should be angry but not sin and do not let the sun go down without addressing our anger (Ephesians 4:26, NIV). Anger can come suddenly or it can come slowly but when anger is not dealt with promptly it can build up and can be like placing a potato in the tailpipe of a car, sitting in the car in a garage breathing in all the carbon monoxide and slowly dying. Anger can take such a root in us it becomes sin alone because in order to build anger up concerning someone who has offended us, hurt us, or even betrayed us it would amount to unforgiveness. We are supposed to forgive others because we are forgiven by Christ (Ephesians 4:32, NIV). Sometimes, our situations may vary for some people it is easier to forgive and for some people it is easier to forget and some people may be able to do both and some do neither. Either way, sometimes we just have to go before God and ask Him to help us to forgive others as we remember we are yet forgiven. Eventually, it becomes an honor to forgive others although we may experience our own processes of being delivered completely from those situations which the enemy tries to use to hold us hostage in and bind us up in our own anger chain. When we promptly handle our anger or whenever we give our anger to God is when He begins to counsel us and deliver us from the anger which had us bound. If a person offends us the best way to handle the situation the Bible mentions is to go to that person and speak with them (Matthew 18:15-17, NIV), give that person a peace offering and that can be done by making peace with that person which will bless you mightily (Matthew 5:9, NIV). There have been times when I could have been angry at someone or the same person for various reasons at various times but after I made peace with that person I felt so much better inwardly. As we get closer to God the one of the best positives about forgiveness and making peace is blessing the other person. It does not matter if they lack knowledge concerning our peacemaking, forgiveness or not because it is always about the long-term results and outcome. It is a possibility that we are the only ones which receive immediate release from the situation because that person could still be holding onto anger and unforgiveness. Letting go of the anger releases the bitterness or resentment which has built up within us during the time we held on to anger. Bitterness and resentment complement each other and are co-partners with anger and are also just as dangerous. But just like a bitter lemon we can make lemonade and afterwards it taste really good and especially for all the lemonade lovers. So, whether others choose to survive and forgive and be released of anger, bitterness and resentment or not once it is accomplished in our lives we are headed for growth and so much more, freedom. Anger, bitterness, resentment and unforgiveness is a like being in prison and it is up to us to choose whether we want a lifetime sentence or not. We do not have to be stuck in prison because God is able to deliver us from anger, bitterness, resentment and unforgiveness.

Pride

Pride is a spirit which can knock on the door of our hearts and we can let pride in knowingly or unknowingly but either way pride comes to take over our house just as a home invader would go a try to take over people in their homes. I have suffered with pride on several occasions so the spirit has come back and unknowingly I have let pride right back in my house. To be honest, most times I do not know until it is too late but God is also helping me to know and to be proactive in Him to prevent pride from creeping in and taking over. There are many ways pride comes in our house and God will always be there to reveal the truth to us if we are listening. "When the unclean spirit has gone out of a person, it passes through waterless places seeking rest, and finding none it says, 'I will return to my house from which I came. And when it comes, it finds the house swept and put in order. Then it goes and brings seven other spirits more evil than itself, and they enter and dwell there. And the last state of that person is worse than the first" (Luke 11:24-26, NIV). The workplace is one of those times when pride can come in like a flood because there may not always be harmony in the workplace. There are times where we can become angry at someone or others and then bitterness and resentment begin to settle and become comfortable either suddenly or over a period of time which can vary for each individual. Being humble towards people who we may have offended unintentionally or been offended by, had a disagreement with, being mistreated by a person and so many other workplace issues which can create conflict may not be easy. When we are trying to live our lives according to Gods requirements does not mean pride or any other unclean spirit will not try and come in and make themselves at home. I have suffered obtaining pride in the workplace and God let me know you are walking in pride by letting me fall but not completely "Pride goes before destruction, a haughty spirit before a fall" (Proverbs 16:18, NIV). Sometimes, God will shake us to get us back on track according to His will. It is up to us to obey. Through all the hurt, emotional abuse and so much more in the workplace pride can come in and make us feel like our refuge but God is our refuge, our deliverer and so much more. Pride can only deliver us from those experiences we experience temporarily whether at home, workplace or anywhere dealing with people but when we give it to God in prayer, forgive, humble ourselves and get back in His will we become free once again from the chains the enemy was using to hold us in bondage. So, we can take things in our own hands or remember the nails in Jesus hands and begin to understand just how He has already taken those things in His hands for us to be capable of walking humbly in His sight "Humble yourselves before the Lord, and he will lift you up" (James 4:10, NIV).

Idols

There are many wile tactics the enemy uses to keep Gods children wandering in the wilderness BeHind ScHedule just as he did the Israelites. Having other gods before God which were and still are idols was and is the enemies main wile tactic. Idolatry has many faces and can vary from things as simple as food and sports, not limiting becoming our own idol (self), other persons, materialism and money, one's status and anything we put before God. "You shall have no other gods before me. You shall not make for yourself an image in the form of anything in heaven above or on the earth beneath or in the waters below. You shall not bow down to them or worship them; for I, the Lord your God, am a jealous God, punishing the children for the sin of the parents to the third and fourth generation of those who hate me" (Exodus 20:3-5, NIV). Yes, fourth generation! This is why it is so crucial for the enemy to keep us bound or to bind us in having idols or maintaining idols because he wants our children and future generations to be bound in the same chains over and over again. "Put to death, therefore, whatever belongs to your earthly nature: sexual immorality, impurity, lust, evil desires and greed, which are idolatry" (Colossians 3:5, NIV). The enemy knows us more than we know ourselves and can have us walking in different forms of idolatry for many reasons whether from hurt, disappointment, lack of trust, rebellion and so forth but God is always willing to cleanse us from all unrighteous "If we confess our sins, he is faithful and just and will forgive us our sins and purify us from all unrighteousness" (1 John 1:9, NIV).

Rejection

Rejection is one of the most used weapons of the enemy because he was rejected himself and cast from heaven (Revelation 12:7-9, NIV) because he wanted to take Gods place so he does not use this weapon lightly but mightily! Our God is great and mightier and He takes the good and bad including rejection and continues the good work He began in us until the day of Christ return (Phillipians1:6, NIV). So God remains undefeated even with rejection just like everything else we may have dealt with or deal with. One of the most honorable details about rejection is that Jesus suffered rejection and when we suffer rejection we are able to participate and understand a small depth of His sufferings (1Peter 2:21, NIV). We are also able to understand today what it feels like to God when we reject Him and His son Jesus and choose people, things, idols and so much more over Him. God gave His only son and Jesus died for us and He is still suffering rejection today (John 3:16, NIV).

Rejection is very painful and sometimes it can feel like someone has knocked all the breath out of our bodies, our hearts are being ripped out of our chest, cause anger, sadness, bitterness, ect., controlled only by tears or some type of immediate gratification (drugs, food, sex, shopping are just a few examples). Everyone's experience and ways of dealing with rejection may vary and sometimes can be fatal but many of us have experience rejection in our lifetimes and if rejection can keep its grips in us rejection can control us for a lifetime. Rejection can begin in childhood whether you had both parents and no parents, stem from relationships, and accumulate over the years in the workforce. There are so many other ways to end up dealing with a spirit of rejection which can become a ruling spirit (the main spirit which causes the most damage in life simply speaking) but God will always help us to identify where rejection stemmed from when we are seeking Him. God also delivers us of rejection but we have to do the natural where He can do the supernatural just like if we were trying to lose weight, stop smoking cigarettes, spend more time with our family or read more!

"We have to seek ye the kingdom of heaven first and its righteousness and all the other things shall be added" (Matthew 6:33, NIV). There are a lot of things we may need added in our lives and this scripture is not just talking about material stuff but we need love, joy, peace, wisdom, knowledge and most importantly a relationship with God. We are lost without Him;

He is a lamp unto our feet and a light to our path (Psalm 119:105, NIV). Once the light comes on we realize that rejection is not healthy for us (but God does use it for our good) and it can be so devastating time after time which it can seem like we are rejecting ourselves over and over again by letting the enemy keep his grips in us! The fight is spiritual there is nothing we can do about it but give it to God and He has already taken care of it by giving us His son, Jesus! God leads us to victory with wisdom, knowledge and understanding! The enemy is so jealous of us he knows if he can continue to use his tactics on us and keep us in his territory in many slick ways then we could end up being rejected by God just like he was! The pain and anger alone from rejection can cause bitterness and strife for a lifetime if we let it! "But the Lord said to Samuel, "Do not consider his appearance or his height, for I have rejected him. The Lord does not look at the things people look at. People look at the outward appearance, but the Lord looks at the heart" (1 Samuel 16:6-7, NIV). Whatever it takes today, ask God to help you overcome rejection and be well on your way to healing, deliverance and restoration.

Control

Control is one of many faces which can be very unhealthy for relationships, churches, businesses, cities, states and nations and cause us to be or become behind schedule in the purposes God has for our lives. Control's face is no respecter of persons and it can be your face one day and someone else face another day the enemy is using to do the controlling. Satan does not care who he is using to do the controlling, manipulating and most everything else which comes along with controlling people or situations to have ones way. Whether intentional or unintentional control is control and the only person in control is God. If the enemy can get you to believe anyone is in control except God even yourself satan has won most of the war. It does not matter how in control a person, people, various systems or even satan himself may appear to be they are usually just be out of control because God is always in control no matter what the situation looks like. Remember, satan was so out of control he was kicked out of heaven and he can cause our lives to be so out of control we need God to kick him out of our lives. God is omnipresent and omnipotent and is in control of everything and he only gives the enemy permission to accomplish many things he does but it is only strategically done by God to turn what the enemy means for our bad around for good.

There are various types of ways the enemy can use people to control you and you probably can pinpoint those ways right off but God may have to give you wisdom in the hidden ways you might never notice. While God is setting us free He shines the light on everything but we have to pay attention, stay in the light and take heed to its directions. People can try and control you or a situation you maybe currently going through based on their perceptions of your or the situation but God knows the intentions and motives of the hearts. Many people have problems obtaining good employment because of past mistakes, not enough experience these days and so much more. People do not realize they are missing out on hiring very talented people whom are just like them, human because they are controlled by the past and prejudice. God is able to judge you or any situation better than man can so when people judge you and misunderstand you based on what they see or even hear thank God that He is all knowing!

Going back in time, Hitler's zeal came from the power he obtained through controlling millions during the Holocaust and that control caused him to kill millions and destroy many peoples loved ones and their future generations. Hitler's agenda was based on eliminating a people he did not value and believe to be of any importance but he was so blinded he did not understand we are all important to our creator God. Control can be a very evil power and can and has caused many lives to be destroyed including your own maybe in various ways but sometimes it's not only control which the destroys one's life but the lack of knowledge concerning how control can or has played a part in one's own life.

Going ahead now, talking about the Tribulation and the mark of the beast, which is the numbers 666. During this seven year time period people will not be able to buy sell or trade without the mark of the beast, the antichrist. Their lives will be controlled either way because the people who choose then to serve God will either be killed, in hiding or option to give up during this time because of the control the antichrist will have over their lives. The others who take of the mark of the beast will have sold their souls and will not have the second chance to enter heaven but will have given their souls over to be able to live comfortably probably the way they are living now or the way they have always wanted to live. The antichrist is not going to make the choice as easy as Jesus has made the choice now. So, it is better to seek Gods face now and let Jesus be Lord of our lives now than have to suffer the terrible injustice during that period when Jesus has already paid the price for us to be free.

Satan will use to people or situations to try and control a person or people of value or importance just as Hitler did and as the antichrist will because the antichrist knows we are very important to God but the antichrist will treat people like a second hand slave and manipulate their freedom to feel important because satan lost his importance in heaven when he tried to take God's place in heaven. We have to always remember we are important to God no matter how others treat us, humiliate us and more just as Jesus which was persecuted and crucified! We also have to remember who we are in Christ and share the Gospel of Christ with others so they will know God sacrificed His only son where He could be Lord over our lives and we would not have to settle for the future of the antichrist's attempt to be lord over our lives, our loved ones lives or others' lives. God deserves the Glory over all lives!

Do you have any puppeteers in your life? Those puppeteers may be in your workplace, home, church or even society but satan is the master puppeteer. When it comes down to using people to try and control and manipulate your life or circumstances and outcomes concerning your life satan is the master puppeteer controlling your puppeteer. Jesus is the Lord of Lords and the King of Kings and wants to be Lord of our lives but satan is the master puppeteer of the puppeteers. Satan only wants to only steal, kill and destroy our lives from our worth, to our promises and destinies in Christ Jesus. No matter whom satan is using to be the puppeteer in your life whether the puppeteers intentions and motives are intentional or unintentional due to complexes whether spiritual, emotional or both either can be harmful to your present and future and mostly because those strings can affect the choices you make. As the puppeteer is controlling your life in many ways they are unaware in most cases because of complete, partial or even temporary spiritual blindness they are also being controlled.

They are being controlled by a force of darkness even greater than themselves and to a higher degree if they are not in Christ or seeking His righteousness (Matthew 6:33, NIV). If the puppeteer is in Christ and still dealing with issues of the heart that puppeteer can overcome because greater is He which is in them than he that is in the world (1 John 4:4, NIV). Satans tactics is to use people who have a weak or a willing spirit which we all have been there and if not cautious and become knowledgeable can most likely fall short of Gods glory anytime. The most important key is having knowledge and understanding what those triggers are or what their triggers are because the spirit may be willing to overcome but the flesh is weak. Also, try not to remain in that mode or remain under another's mode during those circumstances because of the various outcomes which can derive from what was intentional or unintentional. Satan has to be able to control a puppeteer based on the use of ones emotions, feelings stemming from jealousy, hatred and more which tends to invite wickedness and evilness on the scene. This is contrary to Gods spirit and His characteristics which He wants us to develop in spiritually and those characteristics are the fruits of the spirits not wicked or evil spirits (Galatians 5:22-23, NIV). The enemy knows wickedness and evil spirits only keep one spiritually blind which can potentially deprive one of walking in Christ at all or the fullness of God.

Whether one is walking in Christ or not walking in Christ, God can turn what satan came to steal, kill and destroy around for good as both make a choice or choose to love God (Romans 8:28, NIV). Also, satan is still helping all people involved whether puppet or puppeteer past, present and future because God can and always bring an open and willing vessel who is diligently seeking Him into knowledge of the truth. If you are open, God will begin to show you what's going on in the darkness in your life and you will begin to see the light. You will realize God is actually in control and to gain control over your life or gain back control the enemy has used one to deprive you of slightly or greatly will take discipline which is also a fruit of the spirit, self-control. In many cases we have fed fires in our lives with fire because of the lack of knowledge whether in the workplace, home, church or within society.

Many of us have made Jesus Lord of our lives but still sometimes are fighting fire with fire as we either wrestle with, or have wrestled with being controlled or trying to control others lives, situations or both in life. There are other spirits which contribute to the controlling issues one may be dealing with in life and one of those roles is recognized as the Jezebel spirit. In the Bible, Jezebel is a woman but her spirit exists today and tries to reign in woman or man. Jezebel was controlling and possessed evil spirits (2 Kings 9, NIV). Most people today associate Jezebel with the wearing lipstick or make-up but God looks inward while man looks outward and there are far many more spiritual deficiencies such as the evil spirits Jezebel portrayed than make-up or lipstick! Those deficiencies derive from the lack of knowledge, lack of growth or stagnation concerning developing the fruits of the spirits which is another reason the Body of Christ is always subject to the Jezebel spirit just as the kingdom of darkness, the world. The Jezebel spirit just like any other spirit is no respecter of person and does not care whom is devoured because those spirits are only seeking for a host (1 Peter 5:8, NIV). Has your back ever been against the wall and frustration set in or maybe you had to make a decisions to do the right thing but you were angry? That could possibly be the Jezebel spirit and once those decisions have been made those spirits and possibly the Jezebel spirit has gotten the victory over the situation. This is one reason the fruit of the spirit, discipline is so vital along with all the other fruits to help get us past so many limitations which try and keep us behind schedule. The enemy's main goal is to keep you behind schedule and from walking into the plans God has for your life where he can remain in control of your life forever. The side effect to the enemy's goal is not only to remain in control of your life but to be capable of controlling your future generations lives too!

In Christ, He will tug at our spirits sending us the spirit of truth to help us when the flesh is tugging on the other end trying to get us to make the wrong decisions. That is why it is so important to make the Jesus Lord of our lives but we also have to choose to do the right things. God loves us to so much He gave us an option to choose Him and also gave us an option of freewill. This is where we do not have to choose the perfect will God planned for our lives which is exactly what the enemy counts on to keep us and our generations from our predestined lives.

God is not a God of control but allows us to have free-will but He does desire us to walk in His perfect will. He knows the enemy comes to steal, kill and destroy as you can choose to walk freely through life not seeking God concerning any area of your life. So therefore, since God is not a controlling God, He does not like how the enemy comes in to control our lives but will allow it as He helps us or we decide to seek His perfect will for our lives. If we choose freewill over perfect will or make no decisions at all satan would try to keep us walking in circles or whatever the wilderness maybe concerning our lives year after year. It is very important for you to come into knowledge whether or not you are controlling or allowing others to control you or situations concerning you.

The enemy would allow a premeditation type of control to occur to where others or you may not recognize it is premeditation. Satan will have one thinking they are getting away with various wicked or evil acts not caring or understanding that God knows everything. Also, there is a reaction to every action and that reaction may just very well show up in your own life somewhere down the line when you least expect it. The enemy does not fight fair when you think you are fighting against another that is when satan is only using them or you and in a slick way is fighting against them or you. That is his tactic to steal, kill and destroy whatever his objective is concerning your life or theirs at that time and it is only designed to keep everyone behind schedule. God allows many things to occur in our lives which are also meant to counterattack the past, present and future attacks of satan to help us as individuals, families, communities, churches, states, countries and nations to prosper in Him. So, while the enemy may get you to believe a lie temporarily the truth will eventually set you free because there is nothing new under the sun and everything hidden will be revealed.

It's not a secret! Powers, principalities and spiritual wickedness in high places have been controlling people and circumstances forever and don't want to give up their strength. As a people, we have to give up those areas of weaknesses where we are being controlled or being controlling and begin to trust in God in those situations and His grace is sufficient (2 Corinthians 12:9, NIV). Powers, principalities and spiritual wickedness in high places are not going to relinquish control because it's spiritual which is how those powers and principalities continue to get their strength. Powers and principalities also continue to become stronger when and if we allow those powers and principalities to remain. We have to resist satan where he will flee and if not in most cases when we are resistant to change those same situations or circumstances will push us towards repentance. Once we are pushed toward repentance then we also come into the same conclusion as if we had made the choice freely to resist satan and that conclusion being satan is not letting go, we have to let go and let God.

We do not struggle against flesh and blood but against rulers, against authorities, against powers of this dark world, and against spiritual forces of evil in the heavenly places (Ephesians 6:12, NIV). The war is real it is and that means you are in a war it is up to you who wins the war but satan has been in war a long time and you can't win the war alone. Jesus died and has actually already won the war for you and as you make Him or you already have may have made Him Lord of your life then you can trust Him to bring you out of darkness into His marvelous light. There is a process and you have to do the natural and Jesus will do the supernatural because Jesus does not just come into our lives and strip us of our freewill! He loves us that much but it's about choice. We have to choose which God we are going to serve and then the beat goes on (Joshua 24:15, NIV)! You do not have to be the puppet or the puppeteer in your life or anyone else's life because Jesus desires to set you free from everything which has held you captive in your life and use the past to be the bridge to your future. You do not have to allow satan to continue being a puppeteer or using others to be a puppeteer in your life as you begin to walk in knowledge and freedom. Go ahead and start walking over YOUR bridge! You can do all things in Christ which strengthen you (Philippians 4:13, NIV)!

Yes Lord!

Through all of life's challenges we have always had a choice. We have always had the right to choose whether we would let the trials and tribulations of life make us or break us and especially when we obtained knowledge that those situations could have devastating outcomes. There is a quote by (Lee) which says, "A quitter never wins and a winner never quits" and many have stood on this quote just as if it were the word of God. We see a winner in Jesus and He was and still is our biggest example! Jesus did not stay on the boat but He walked on the water. Jesus lived thirty three years on this earth and it was not in vain, he walked His journey out and fulfilled His purpose which God had ordained for His life. Jesus walked on water and hung on the cross, went to hell and back becoming, rose on the third day becoming our Savior where we would obtain His spirit being born into a world of sin with odds against us. God gave His only begotten Son.(John 3:16, NIV). By obtaining Jesus spirit, the spirit of truth, we became the righteousness of God (even when we are wrong we are right) and are capable by His spirit which is greater within us to walk a righteous life (yielding to His spirit and walking in spirit and truth) during our journeys. He defeated the plans the enemy had for our lives and future generations. Jesus obtained His prize which was the high call, walked on water fulfilling his purpose as He departed and arrived on time.

God brought Jesus to it and brought Him through it and Jesus came out victorious when the tomb had been rolled back. We have all experienced, the God bringing us to the "fear factors" and bringing us through the "fear factor" moments to achieve great victories by Christ Jesus for God's glory!

Jesus did not stay on the boat feeling defeated because of the hand which was being dealt to Him at this time and He surely didn't stay on the boat and wait for it to sink. Jesus walked on water the same as God expects us to walk on water "spiritual waters" and trust that the Lord is holding our hands during those times of trials and tribulations. God expects us to trust in Him to split our "Red Seas" and carry us through the storms of life. He doesn't want us to shipwreck, sink or drown on our journeys but He wants us to survive and get the prize and reach our destinies! We all were created by God with a purpose to fulfill and a cross to carry just as Mary (virgin mother) and her son Jesus (our Savior). God does not want the challenges of life to keep us on the boat and not fulfill our purpose and walk into our destinies. God wants us to walk on water because He is the water! God does not want us to let anything easily beset us too long because the enemy's goal is to abort and destroy the purpose which He has placed on the inside of each and every last of us.

It is time to walk on water even though there may have been a late departure, God is our captain and He will make sure we arrive to where He has destined for us to arrive. Are you ready to get to your God-given destination and leave the destinations satan disguised as the final destination? It has to be an internal yes! Once, you get out of the boat and begin to walk on water, God begins to take you all the way to shore! Trust in the Lord with all your heart and lean not to your own understanding but acknowledge Him in all your ways and He will direct your paths. (Proverbs 3:5-6, NIV). You were born with a purpose now get off the boat!

God Bless You

Malvnda Barbee

Then he said to them all: "If anyone would come after me, he must deny himself and take up his cross daily and follow me.

Luke 9:23

Printed in the United States
By Bookmasters